God vs. Money
Participant Guide

J. Clif Christopher

God
★ ★ vs. ★ ★
Money

Winning Strategies in the Combat Zone

Abingdon Press

Nashville

GOD VS. MONEY PARTICIPANT GUIDE:
WINNING STRATEGIES IN THE COMBAT ZONE

Copyright © 2019 by Abingdon Press

All rights reserved.

Library of Congress Cataloging-in-Publication Data has been requested.

ISBN 978-1-5018-9157-1

Scripture quotations unless noted otherwise are from the Common English Bible. Copyright © 2011 by the Common English Bible. All rights reserved. Used by permission. www.CommonEnglishBible.com.

19 20 21 22 23 24 25 26 27 28—10 9 8 7 6 5 4 3 2 1
MANUFACTURED IN THE UNITED STATES OF AMERICA

★ ★ ★

Contents

★ ★ ★

Introduction

Welcome to this group study of the book *God vs. Money: Winning Strategies in the Combat Zone.* This study is for finance teams, stewardship committees, church councils, and other ministry groups responsible for financial decisions in the church. It is for clergy, staff, and laity.

Together you will go through a six-session process, ending with the creation of a yearlong financial plan for your church. This experience will challenge you—both individually and as a ministry team. You will grow and learn, perhaps in unexpected ways. Ultimately, this study should move you toward deeper discipleship. And it should move your congregation toward greater generosity and more complete mission fulfillment.

A Few Important Details

- Plan to complete the study over a period of six to eight weeks.

- Allow one and a half to two hours for each session, except the final session.

- Each participant will need a copy of the main book, *God vs. Money*, and a copy of this participant guide.

- There is space in this book for participants to make notes and to write some brief reflections. Some participants may also wish to have a separate journal or notebook.

- The final session is a group retreat.

  - Allow a full day, minimum, for the retreat.

  - The best format is a five-hour day followed by three hours the next morning.

The Weekly Session Format

Participants are to do assigned reading from the main book, *God vs. Money: Winning Strategies in the Combat Zone*, before arriving for each session. After participants arrive each week, you may begin by praying, sharing joys and concerns, singing a hymn, or participating in another gathering activity. The sessions generally follow this order:

1. Review and discuss the Digging Deeper research activity.

2. View the video.

3. Individually, read the section Understanding the Main Themes.

4. Individually, consider the Individual Reflection questions, writing responses in this guide or in a separate journal or notebook.

5. Gather back together for group discussion. Use the notes pages at the back of the book to write down ideas from your discussion that you may want to include in your Generosity Battle Plan.

6. Assign the Digging Deeper research activity.

7. Make note of the week's homework.

8. Close by reading the Prayer aloud in unison.

Your Final Session:
The God vs. Money Retreat

At or (preferably) before your first session, set the dates, times, and location for the final session, which is a group retreat and requires six to eight hours. Communicate the information to participants so they can make arrangements to attend this crucial final session. The retreat culminates the study, bringing together all of the information you have gathered. At this session you will review all you have learned and discussed during the study. You'll draw conclusions, set priorities, and identify next steps. You will, during the final hours of the retreat, formulate a concrete action plan, your church's personalized Generosity Battle Plan, for the year ahead.

Facilitating This Study

Facilitation of the study is easy and can be handled by one person or rotated among several members of the group. The notes here, and this participant guide, are all you will need. The study is self-directed: simply follow the questions and prompts in this guide. A few reminders for the facilitator:

- Review each week's lesson ahead of time.

- Pay close attention to the Digging Deeper and Participant Homework sections, and make sure the resources required for these activities are available in advance.

- Arrive early to set up and test the video before the session begins.

- Gather any supplies you'd like to have for the session—flip charts, pencils, copies of budget documents, or snacks, for instance.

- Decide in advance with the group how volunteers for the Digging Deeper research will be selected each week.

A Few Notes about the Videos

The videos are an essential component of the study. You'll watch one video during each session. Viewing times range from about six to twelve minutes. The videos feature Clif Christopher in conversation about key points in *God vs. Money*. Talking with Horizons Stewardship Communications Strategist, Len Wilson, Clif shares stories from his own military service and ministry, and his unique brand of down-to-earth inspiration for financial decision-makers in the church. The DVD and streaming videos are available for purchase at http://www.cokesbury.com/god-vs-money.

For each session you will need:

- A DVD player and the *God vs. Money* DVD

—OR—

- A reliable internet connection and a way to view the streaming videos

One Final Suggestion

Consider making this God vs. Money study an annual or biennial commitment. Creating and implementing a finance and stewardship plan is not a one-time-only process. Your congregation, leadership, and community all experience change each year. Your finance and steward-ship plans should change too.

May God lead and bless the conversations you have, the discoveries you make, and the plans you design as a result of this group study. May you, as individuals and as a congregation, grow toward deeper disciple-ship and more powerful ministry in Christ's name!

S e s s i o n   1

The Battle with Money

Read the introduction and chapter 1 of the main book,

God vs. Money: Winning Strategies in the Combat Zone,

before starting this session.

Watch Video 1:
The Battle with Money

Notes:

Understanding the Main Theme

Part of the motivation for this book came from a conversation with an active church layperson nearly twenty years ago. All of the people involved in the conversation had sons who were about to finish school and start their adult lives. Like most parents, we had aspirations for our children. For three of us, those aspirations centered around money, position, comfortability, or living situation. For one, it centered around the idea that a generous life was the life one should most strive for and the sort of life that would bring true joy—regardless of income, house size, or position in life. This father wanted his son to be "a tither." It was one of those moments when I became speechless.

This dad did not mean that he just wanted his son to give 10 percent of his income away and then not worry about the other 90 percent. He used the phrase "a tither" to communicate his hope that his son would put his trust and full confidence in God and not in stuff. He was using the term *tithe* as a reference to the larger word *generous*. It made me think through my own priorities and that which I seek not only for my children but also for myself. It became a defining moment in my life. It also bothered me that I had not clearly heard this message from my church, nor had I adequately taught it while a pastor—and yet, it seemed fundamental to our faith.

Then I began to explore where our priorities were and whether our strivings were moving us closer or farther away from a relationship with our Creator. In America especially, we have an enormous amount of discretionary income beyond that needed for food, shelter, and clothing. The amounts we choose to spend on toys, jewelry, gambling, and even pornography stun me. None of those things will even come close to bringing us lasting joy and peace. Yet, we continue to believe that one more car or one more raise or one more title will somehow make us happy.

The statistics on the faith of Americans seem to show that whatever we have been doing in the church has not been very convincing. Membership is down, attendance in worship is down, belief in the Bible is down. The message of Jesus may still be very strong, but the delivery services seem to be suffering mightily in getting the Word out.

This past year, my wife and I took a trip to Europe to visit many of the great capitals of the world. In every one of these ancient cities, we saw numerous tall steeples over some of the most gorgeous churches we had ever seen. The stained glass was breathtaking. The gold and brass trim glistened. Organ pipes stood by the thousands, connected to four and five rank organs. The problem was that almost all of these churches were empty. I could not help but wonder whether this is the future of the faith in America.

All of this gave me a sense of urgency—a feeling that we simply cannot wait for the next generation to tackle this problem. This is a fight that I should engage in and a fight that the *present* church should lead. We simply cannot wait any longer.

Individual Reflection

When it comes to generosity or money, we generally shy away from conversation about it. We consider it personal, and some even think of it as "dirty." It is out of bounds. However, if we are going to help solve this problem within the church, and thus the world, reflection must begin with each of us as individuals.

Use the space provided in this chapter to write your own thoughts and responses to the questions below. If you prefer, you can do your writing in a separate notebook or journal.

★ What did you think when you read that one father wanted his son to be "a tither" first and foremost? How would you have responded to the question about your aspirations for your child?

★ What does your answer tell you about yourself?

★ Do you feel any sense of urgency of action or making serious changes as is described in these chapters? Does the use of battlefield language resonate with you as to how serious the situation is?

★ Do you feel that generosity is a core value of your church's life? Is it a word that is used much in preaching or in classes?

Group Discussion

Discuss your thoughts about the questions above as a group. Depending upon the size of your group, you may want to talk in a circle or around a table all together. If more than five or six people are at this session, you might break up into groups of two to four. Share together, as you feel led, your answers to the above questions. Take about five minutes for each one.

Group Learning

What specifically have you learned that you want to incorporate into the Generosity Battle Plan this group will be creating as you move forward? Discuss and decide together.

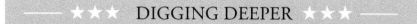

★★★ DIGGING DEEPER ★★★

Designate someone in the group to speak to the pastor or financial secretary and get an estimate of how many tithing families there are in your church.

The same person (or a different person) can research the average household income for your zip code, area, or town and see how many families give at a rate that would be 10 percent or more of that average. Then figure out what the giving to the church would be if all family units gave at that average and what might possibly be done with the extra income to the church.

Assign someone to bring a copy of the church budget to the next session.

PARTICIPANT HOMEWORK

★ ★

Spend time with those who live in your household discussing what tithing would look like and whether it should be a goal for your family.

If you already consider yourself a tither (giver of 10 percent of gross income), what would Christian generosity look like for you? Write here or in your journal your thoughts about this question and the discussion you have with your family.

Read chapters 2 and 3 of the main book.

Prayer

Lord, thank you for creating us and for creating all that is. Thank you for trusting us to be your stewards and to use the gifts of this world as you would have us do. Forgive us for failing to fully live up to your confidence in us and trying to act like all things belong to us and not to you. Help us, through this experience, to grow as your disciple and to learn how to lead others to do the same. In the name of your greatest gift, Jesus Christ, amen.

Session 2

Leadership, Integrity, and a Preview of the Battle Plan

Read chapters 2 and 3 of the main book,

God vs. Money: Winning Strategies in the Combat Zone,

before this session.

Digging Deeper Review

During the first ten minutes of your session, discuss what was learned by the activities following last week's session. Begin with a brief report from the person who did the giving research. That person should share what was found and should summarize the implications of the findings regarding your congregation's level of generosity.

Can you fully do the mission God has called you to do with the resources available?

A few people should share what they wrote in their journal about tithing and generosity.

What was the discussion like with your family? Did anyone struggle with this?

Watch Video 2: The Battle Plan

This video explains a key *God vs. Money* concept— the importance of a yearlong Generosity Battle Plan. The battle plan is a main objective for this study, and together as a group you will design one in your last session. The video will help you begin to think about the battle plan now, and every upcoming lesson will build toward that objective.

Notes:

Understanding the Main Themes

In these two chapters I dealt with two primary themes: leadership and stewardship.

Integrity is defined as an adherence to moral and ethical principles, soundness of moral character, or honesty. It is a trait that most expect from their leaders. We want our doctors, teachers, judges, pastors, and yes, even politicians to have integrity. It often makes the newspapers when any of these leaders is caught not exemplifying integrity. Now, it would be hoped that all people in every type of job would show integrity, but followers are never expected to rise to the level of leaders. Using military examples, there are different levels of defined expectations for a new private than for a commissioned or noncommissioned officer.

In the church, the pastor IS the leader. No one else is asked to stand and speak for God once a week while everyone else sits and listens. It is a humbling and awesome responsibility and must be done with the highest levels of integrity. Lay leaders, board members, deacons, elders, and other designated persons set aside to lead a congregation must also bring a higher level of integrity to their roles. No one *has* to be a pastor, and no one *has* to accept a role of leadership in a congregation, but if you do say yes then you have accepted a higher calling that demands a higher level of integrity.

Have you ever heard a player say, "We would run through a brick wall for our coach"? I have played on teams that had this attitude about their coach, and I have served in military units that felt this way about their leaders. These are teams and units that see all the best qualities in their leader. They see the leader doing everything he or she can to make success possible. As a player or a soldier, you do not want to be the weak link that lets the leader down. You want to be the best you can be.

In the church, sometimes our leaders seem to care much more about being a buddy than being a leader. They do not want to ask too much of us or challenge us to go beyond. Oftentimes, this is because they do not want to be challenged themselves, and from their leader platform they can dictate the effort expected of others instead. In the church, these are leaders who seem to care more about how another person may feel about them than about how God might feel. They show that they are really working for the backslaps of people rather than the accolades of God.

For pastors and laypersons to truly lead, they must have two things: an understanding of the God-given mission and an authentic theology of stewardship. Only about one in ten of the churches that I work with can tell me what the mission of their church is. They worship every week, have programs throughout the week, and hope to raise hundreds of thousands of dollars—and yet they do not know the answer to *Why?*

If you asked pastors or lay leaders to define Christian stewardship, most would say something like, "It is raising money for the church." The typical view is that the stewardship committee has one job, which is to run the annual fund campaign and raise money for the budget. Many pastors and other leaders see no connection between the ministry of stewardship and the creation of disciples. They may talk about giving 10 percent but never think about the responsibility we all have for using the other 90 percent with integrity as well.

These two chapters are probably the two most important ones in this book if you are a leader within the church. These chapters deal with the foundations your work must be built upon. You must personally accept that as a leader you have a higher calling to serve with integrity in your own personal discipleship in keeping the church body focused on its mission from God. It is OK for you to respond right now with "I do not want this job." In fact, it is better for the church if you would simply say so now than to serve without full integrity later. But, if you stay in, you must develop a strong understanding of the mission you are to lead and of how being a steward is a vital part of how you lead others to do that mission.

Particularly in the third chapter and in the video, I discuss the implications of knowing and communicating the mission to the congregation. It was what everything centered on while I was in a combat theater, and it should be what a congregation rallies around on a daily basis. But this implies that people actually know the mission.

Chapter 2 focused mostly on *why* and *how* leaders must lead. It should be the leaders who most fully understand the mission objectives. They are the ones who should be putting people and resources together to fulfill that mission. And they are the ones who should be exemplifying to all what is required to get the mission done.

Individual Reflection

Use the space provided in this chapter to write your own thoughts and responses to the questions below. If you prefer, you can do your writing in a separate notebook or journal.

NOTE: The person assigned to bring a copy of the budget to this session will share it with the team for this exercise.

★ Does your church share a missional or narrative budget with the members or are you still used to sharing a line item budget?

★ Take a look at the church's budget. As you review the document, what does it tell you about your mission priorities? Is this what you want it to say?

★ Does it bother you for leaders to have a different set of expectations than members have?

★ Is it right for people to expect their pastor to "show and tell" a discipled life?

★ Is it wrong for a pastor to strive for lay leaders who have high integrity in their discipleship and stewardship?

★ Would it make a difference if all board members agreed to a covenant of exemplary generosity and participation in the church?

★ As you go through your life with your wallet and checkbook and credit cards, does it ever dawn on you that what you do with each of those things requires a Christian understanding of stewardship?

Group Discussion

Discuss your thoughts about the questions above as a group. Depending upon the size of your group, you may want to talk in a circle or around a table all together. If more than five or six people are at this session, you might break up into groups of two to four. Share together, as you feel led, your answers to the above questions. Take about five minutes for each one.

Group Learning

What specifically have you learned that you want to incorporate into your Generosity Battle Plan going forward? Discuss and decide together.

★★★ DIGGING DEEPER ★★★

Designate one or more persons in the group to visit with various staff persons or lead volunteers at your church and ask them the questions below. Aim to visit with persons who are responsible for worship, Christian education, adult discipleship, congregational care, outreach, and evangelism. Make notes about what you hear from each person.

1. What are the greatest needs, as you see them, in your particular area of ministry? What is the core human need that drives your work?

2. What are some of the strategies and tactics you use in order to meet these needs?

3. Can you tell me about the people from the congregation and community who are directly involved in this ministry?

Now, take a look at the church's budget, and focus on the areas of ministry you discussed with the staff or other leaders.

Review the notes from your conversations with ministry leaders, and compare them to the budget. Does a story emerge from the conversations you had? From the budget document? How do they compare? Which storytelling "method" will have the greatest impact on your congregation? Why?

What does this tell you about how your church might communicate with the congregation about ministry funding?

PARTICIPANT HOMEWORK

★ ★

Consider whether you would prefer to be a leader or a follower within the church and why.

What might change in the way your church runs if leaders agreed to and followed a leadership covenant?

Write one paragraph in your journal about what money means to you.

Read chapters 4 and 5 of the main book.

Prayer

Lord God, like many people in the Bible, we are not sure we are grateful to be called into leadership. We do not always feel worthy or capable. We are not at all sure we want the responsibility. Help us to discern not only what you want of us but also how we might be faithful in doing it. We pray for our pastor(s). Their role in leading all of us is a difficult one. Bring wisdom, courage, and understanding to them that they may bring such to us. In the name of the greatest leader, Jesus Christ, amen.

★ ★ ★

Session 3

Shifting Attitudes and Setting Expectations

Read chapters 4 and 5 of the main book,

God vs. Money: Winning Strategies in the Combat Zone,

before this session.

Digging Deeper Review

During the first ten minutes of your session, the person(s) who completed this week's Digging Deeper activity should share what was learned about spending in the areas of worship, education, care, and evangelism. Those persons might then share their own thoughts about spending and about how spending is communicated to the congregation. Make notes below and then, as a group, discuss the questions on the following page:

What would you be better off sharing with the congregation, and why?

A. The cost of individual ministry areas, and the key objectives that are achieved through this spending?

B. The salaries and benefits of the people involved in leading and running those ministry areas?

Did anyone think or write about how leaders should lead in your church and what it would mean if there were a leadership covenant? Discuss your thoughts.

Watch Video 3: The Mission Objective

In this video, Clif mentions a sample missional budget, which can be found on page 107 of his book *Not Your Parents' Offering Plate.*

Notes:

Understanding the Main Themes

In chapter 4, I note that our rule of engagement as the church is "where we see sin, we attack it from as many fronts as is necessary to defeat it so that God's kingdom may come upon the earth." If I am not careful, I may find myself sounding like the nineteenth-century preacher standing on a stump waving his Bible as he shouts condemnation about the evils of the society around him. This is not someone most of us would pause long to listen to, but you have to give the person credit for sincere beliefs.

We do not even use the word *sin* much anymore. Of the dozens of sermons I hear every year from a variety of pulpits around the country, I could count on one hand the number of times I have heard the word *sin*. The word *sin* is just not popular anymore. We might say that a certain behavior was not nice or loving or appropriate, but we would rarely call it sin. We might say that we should not do something but it is unlikely we call it sin. *Sin* implies that an action is counter to the will of God and pushes us farther away from a relationship with God. If you choose to steal money that belongs to someone else rather than work for it yourself, it pushes you farther away from the person God wants you to become. It is a sin! If you choose intimacy with a person other than the one you committed to in marriage, it ruins the marriage relationship and the relationship with God. It is a sin! If you give more time and energy to your own wants and desires than to your children, it ruins the parental relationship and your relationship with God. It is a sin! If you give money the power to control your life, if your decisions are based on how you can acquire more and more stuff, then you have begun to worship things and not the Creator. God cannot relate to you. It is a sin!

It is time we proclaimed the sin of materialism loudly and unashamedly. We all choose what to pour ourselves into, where to focus our thoughts and desires. We can choose well or very badly. Love of money is the bad choice festering in the hearts and minds of most people in most congregations. It is the preferred bad choice of our time, far more than any other. That's saying a lot when you consider the vast array of bad choices we can make.

Why are we embarrassed or afraid to work as hard as possible to separate people from that which they love more than God, to help them stop making this very bad choice?

In chapter 5, I talk about the various pieces that must be a part of the church for it to defeat the sin of materialism and save the souls of its congregants. I lifted up Lyle Schaller's quote offered shortly before he passed away, that "90% of all Christian congregations . . . will not be able to compete" for the charitable dollar going forward (*God vs. Money*, page 38). I totally agree with Dr. Schaller and believe that the prime reason churches will lose the war against materialism is that we have so watered down discipleship that few of our "soldiers" know what victory requires.

Throughout the four Gospels we can find one reference after another of what the life of a disciple looks like. That should not surprise us because that is the only thing Jesus called anyone to be—a disciple. The entire Sermon on the Mount, given early in his ministry, was intended to instruct those who thought following Jesus would be cool, to describe for them the reality of discipleship. Jesus wanted them (and us) to know exactly what that followership—that discipleship—was to look like.

In today's church, discipleship is rarely mentioned to visitors and newcomers. If people are breathing then they can "join up." This low level of expectation is the prime reason we see a low level of participation, giving, and serving. We have handed out membership cards with no strings attached. Rotary Club and Boy Scouts express much stricter expectations than the vast majority of churches. In doing this, we have minimized the importance and seriousness discipleship demands and created churches full of people who do not have a clue as to why they are there or why attending, giving, and serving are important. I am convinced that before anyone ever joins a church they should attend a series of classes where the expectations of discipleship are fully explained and laid out for people to accept or reject.

Individual Reflection

Use the space provided in this chapter to write your own thoughts and responses to the questions below. If you prefer, you can do your writing in a separate notebook or journal.

★ Would you like to hear the word *sin* mentioned more often in worship? Should our preaching and classes teach more about what sin is and isn't?

★ What do you think of the suggestion that the love of material things and money is the primary force preventing most people from being in a fuller relationship with God?

★ Think back to churches you've been part of before this one. What do you remember learning about the life of committed discipleship?

★ Were you challenged to a stronger, more complete spiritual life or just welcomed into a new group?

★ Was there more emphasis on the benefits of a Christian life or on how challenging and rewarding it would be?

★ Were any benchmarks discussed for attendance, serving in missions, giving, or praying?

★ Now consider your current church. Turn to pages 41–42 of the main *God vs. Money* book, and take a look at the Spiritual Training Expectations. How do you think your church's leaders would respond to this being integrated into your new member process? Why do you feel they would be supportive or unsupportive?

★ Do you see your church ready to engage people to truly grow in generosity and as committed disciples? Or is your church by its actions primarily concerned with balancing a budget?

Group Discussion

Discuss your thoughts about the questions above as a group. Depending upon the size of your group, you may want to talk in a circle or around a table all together. If more than five or six people are at this session, you might break up into groups of two to four. Share together, as you feel led, your answers to the above questions. Take about five minutes for each one.

After sharing some of the responses to the previous questions, play Chris Janson's song "Buy Me a Boat." It can be found on YouTube or in a music app. Listen clearly to the words and then discuss whether this is a reflection of your church member's attitudes about money and the church, using the questions below to direct your discussion.

> How can a pastor and lay leaders combat this attitude that acquiring is more important than giving?
>
> Review together how your church is helping people give from all possible ways.
>
> What specifically are you doing to encourage annual, capital, and planned giving every year?
>
> Do you know of persons in your church who have made capital gifts outside the church? What about estate or planned gifts?
>
> How might you help people consider the church for any or all of their gifts?

Group Learning

What specifically have you learned that you want to incorporate into your Generosity Battle Plan going forward? Discuss and decide together.

★★★ DIGGING DEEPER ★★★

Designate someone to contact your denominational foundation, an estate attorney, or Horizons Stewardship and investigate how your church might institute a marketing plan for planned gifts.

Also, find out what planned giving policies are in place and determine whether they need to be created or updated.

Assign someone else to look into what discipleship covenants, if any, exist for those accepting a leadership role in the church. How might you raise the discipleship level within the congregation by raising the discipleship example being set by leaders?

PARTICIPANT HOMEWORK

★ ★

Review the Spiritual Training Expectations (pp. 41–42 in *God vs. Money*) and your own written reflections.

How would you have felt if your pastor had communicated discipleship expectations to you before you joined the church? What might have been different for your own spiritual path—in both positive and negative ways?

Should we bring people into church membership at any time and hope they catch on to the idea of committed discipleship as time goes by? Or, like the Army, should we bring them in knowing little about details but everything about expectations?

Spend some time thinking about these concerns, and jot down any ideas or questions you have. Write out any thoughts about what all this means for your congregation and changes you might want to propose.

Read chapters 6 and 8 of the main book. (You'll read chapter 7 for a later session.)

Prayer

Thank you, Lord, for the church and all that it is called to be. We are humbled to consider that we are to be the hands and feet of Christ. We want to follow Jesus, until it involves a cross or a crown of thorns. *Help us.* As leaders in your church today, show us how we can help other people to follow Christ and be obedient to his word, that your Kingdom may someday reign among us. Amen.

S e s s i o n   4

The Principles of Fundraising and Importance of Relationships

Read chapters 6 and 8 of the main book,

God vs. Money: Winning Strategies in the Combat Zone,

before this session.

Digging Deeper Review

During the first ten minutes of your session, discuss what was learned from the activities following last week's session. Begin with a brief report from the person who did the Digging Deeper work this week.

> What was learned about your planned giving program and efforts to promote it in the congregation? If your program is lacking, discuss a few ideas that could strengthen it.
>
> What was learned about the use of covenants in your church?
>
> What was learned about being a high-expectation church?

Do you feel that there would (or would not) be pushback if you instituted a new approach with higher expectations for members' spiritual growth?

If you believe there would be pushback, what do you think is behind that?

Would people resist because they feel it would not align with God's will for your church, or because higher expectations would be more difficult for them?

Watch Video 4: The Art of Spiritual Combat

Notes:

Understanding the Main Themes

In chapter 6, I shared the story of what it was like in my very first week in my first church to be faced with building a new building and raising all the money to pay for it. I had spent four years in a highly valued denominational college and then three years in one of the finest seminaries on the East Coast. The good people of northwest Arkansas were sure that I had the knowledge to lead this process. After all, none of them had such an education. They were farmers, doctors, lawyers, and businesspeople. I was the "professional church guy." Surely, I would know what to do, they thought.

What they did not know was that, while I did have a strong biblical and theological education, I had absolutely zero training in running a nonprofit. I inherited a $200,000 budget, 300 volunteers, no serious capital in the bank, and an immediate need for a million dollars. I just wanted to preach on Sunday and visit the sick during the week. We were all equally incompetent. The only problem was that I was their leader.

I am convinced that the failure to teach the basic tenets of fundraising is a serious flaw in our professional ministry education. Only about 5 percent of our schools require such classes of their students. If you want your pastor to lead your nonprofit, you may have to seek out ways to provide that person with the educational opportunities to gain such knowledge.

This chapter covers three basic principles of fundraising. *Fundraising* is not a dirty word, by the way. It is done throughout the Scriptures. Pastors and church leaders need to understand that in order to achieve success, relationships and trust are critical. People give to people. A compelling case for how the funds will be used to change lives is a must. Just balancing the budget is not a compelling case. And it is fundamental that our teaching and preaching nurtures in people the understanding that we all need to give. People in our congregations should know with their heads and feel in their hearts the basic truth that our need to give is far more urgent than any institution's needs to receive. Our giving feeds and strengthens our souls. It draws us closer to God and helps us avoid self-compulsion.

Chapter 8 covers the reasons it is important for people in our congregations to step up and stand up for Christ and his church in a way that is clear to others. We need leaders from the pews to take their place out front, to demonstrate their sense of urgency and commitment to giving, to be models for the rest of the congregation—as well as for newcomers and people in the wider community. The committed givers in your church must be like Teddy Roosevelt charging up San Juan Hill. They must have bold confidence and trust that others will have confidence to follow.

Your efforts to grow a congregation full of generous disciples can hinge on your ability to identify and gracefully deploy your most committed givers. Other nonprofit organizations are pursuing these leading givers too. Those organizations often have directors of development, executive directors, or presidents who are well-equipped and highly skilled in cultivation and solicitation. They have strategic programs targeting some of the same people who are the leading givers in your church. Their staffs know what works—how to approach, communicate with, and secure committed donors. These organizations operate purposefully, and their missions are good and important. And too often they outwork the church, receiving abundant resources and commitments from leading givers—some of which those givers might have offered to the church. Pastors and others in church leadership must learn how to cultivate major gifts and eventually ask for those gifts. When pastors do not do this, they put the mission of the church at the back of the line. And, of course, it deserves to be at the front.

Individual Reflection

Use the space provided in this chapter to write your own thoughts and responses to the questions below. If you prefer, you can do your writing in a separate notebook or journal.

★ Thinking back over all the fundraising campaigns you have been a part of, do you feel your church was conscious of the fundraising principles outlined in chapter 6? Or was the approach more of "give because it is your church" request based on obligation?

★ What sort of compelling case can you make right now for why persons should prioritize their gifts to your church?

★ If your pastor set aside time to intentionally cultivate persons who had the capacity to make significant gifts to fund the mission and ministry of your church, would you consider that an appropriate use of the pastor's time or an inappropriate use? Be sure to make your case from a spiritual platform.

★ The argument is being made that we as Christ's people must learn how to compete alongside the 1.5 million nonprofits in America that are cultivating and soliciting donations from people everywhere, including people in our congregations. Could learning how to better compete help you increase your mission and outreach? Or is competing inappropriate in the church?

Group Discussion

Discuss your thoughts about the questions above as a group. Depending upon the size of your group, you may want to talk in a circle or around a table all together. If more than five or six people are at this session, you might break up into groups of two to four. Share together, as you feel led, your answers to the above questions. Take about five minutes for each one.

Group Learning

What specifically have you learned that you want to be sure and incorporate into your Generosity Battle Plan going forward? Discuss and decide together.

——— ★★★ DIGGING DEEPER ★★★ ———

Designate someone to interview the pastor(s) and key staff members to find out how they feel about cultivating relationships with those who can fund the mission of the church. Ask each pastor and staff member the following questions.

1. What are some of your biggest emotional challenges with cultivating relationships with people who can fund the mission of the church?

2. What are some of your biggest practical challenges with cultivating these relationships?

3. What sort of experience and training do you have in this regard? What sort of experience or training might help you in this regard?

4. What records and information do you use in order to identify and work with high-potential givers?

5. If the person you are interviewing is a pastor, ask: Do you have access to all giving records?

6. What do you feel might help you to begin (or improve) cultivating and following through on relationships with high-potential givers?

7. Do you feel this is different than cultivating people who have gifts to sing or teach or lead worship?

Make notes about the thoughts, ideas, and feelings the pastors and staff share with you.

Brainstorm a few ideas for how your committee or team might provide support or practical help for this work.

PARTICIPANT HOMEWORK

★ ★

Make a quick list of the study groups, adult Sunday school classes, and other small groups in your church. Each person in this God vs. Money study should choose one group from the list and agree to interview that group, asking them to discuss this question:

Looking back on your history with this church, when it comes to raising money, what do you feel is usually given the greatest emphasis—the church's practical need for funding or the individual's spiritual need to give?

Listen to people's responses, and make a few notes of the key points.

On your own, write down three ways that your church significantly impacts your community that would be lacking if the church were no longer there.

Read chapter 9 of the main book.

Prayer

Lord, we confess to you that far too often we feel uncomfortable about money that is given to the church. We sometimes view these gifts as unhealthy in some way. We struggle to see money as another blessing you grant us, which we must determine how to use on your behalf. Help us, Lord, through this study to overcome seeing money as just a means to things, and rather to see it as a glorious gift from you, our Creator, that we are blessed to use for your Kingdom's sake. Amen.

If Only . . . Mission, Not Money

Read chapter 9 of the main book,

God vs. Money: Winning Strategies in the Combat Zone,

before this session.

Digging Deeper Review

During the first ten minutes of your session, discuss what was learned from the activities following last week's session. Begin with a brief report from the persons who did the Digging Deeper work this week.

> What was discovered about efforts to intentionally cultivate relationships with major donors, and to follow through with asking for their gifts?
>
> What information, strategies, and tactics do the pastors and others use?
>
> Does your pastor have full access to donor records?
>
> Where do staff need support and practical help?
>
> How has this discovery process with the pastors and others been helpful?

Did you discover anything that would lead you to change any current church practices or policies?

A few people should share their reflections about how previous giving campaigns have been conducted. Discuss that exercise and your reflections as a group.

What is your assessment, as a group, about the congregation's feelings about the giving campaigns? Are the campaigns generally perceived to be about paying the church's bills, or about fostering the members' spiritual growth?

Watch Video 5: The Battleground

Notes:

Understanding the Main Themes

Chapter 9 deals with what I call the Big Guns—the capital campaign. I tried to cover the basic *do*s and *don't*s in this chapter, and I especially wanted all church leaders to hear that we are currently losing out on billions of mission dollars because we do not practice the art of regularly appealing to the capital "pocket" of giving.

This is the storehouse pocket. This is where our investments reside. It is where we hold property, stocks, bonds, insurance policies, and one-time liquidity events like the sale of a business or other valuable asset. We place these proceeds in a different pocket than the one where we pay for groceries and rent or buy clothes and pay the church. They are nowhere near our regular cash flow. They are, however, gifts from God to be used as God would want—just like all other gifts. People do not want to mix these pockets. They will not often even think of what is in this pocket until some one-time special opportunity comes along that they are very interested in. At that time, they will reach into that pocket and make a significant gift over a short period of time to help make the opportunity a reality.

But you say, "We cannot build a building every year. We have sought these gifts before, but only every ten to fifteen years when we need to build or remodel." I hear you, but you misunderstand me here.

I am not suggesting that you should build a new building every year but rather that you should have a bold vision *every day*. Every day the leaders of the church should be looking forward to see what could be, if only… Every day, you should be focused on your church's unique context and mission field, the God-given vision you have for reaching people and transforming lives. Even when you actually need a new building, the emphasis should not be on the brick and mortar but on the difference in people's lives that your building will make possible. The proper emphasis is on responding to God's call to be God's people where you are planted. It is about a dream becoming a reality. That is what we need more of.

It is this message of *what could be* that is shared in worship, in classes, and in emails and other correspondence. The dream of a new youth center. The dream of building a dozen new homes for those who have none. The dream of a hundred new families coming into the church through a new contemporary worship venue. The dream of a sorting center for donated food and clothing for people in need. It is these dreams that should be constantly placed before the people as a hope, if only...

The "only" is the funding required to move a dream off the drawing board and into actual implementation. You must continually paint the picture for people in your church community, reminding them of the possibilities, helping them envision the meaningful and significant things that could occur among and around them. You must connect the dots between those visions of your church's unique mission and the opportunities your congregants have to be part of it. They should see what could happen if they were to provide the funding. This is what we should share throughout the year. When we do, the people who are impassioned by those visions and who also have significant capital pockets may just come forth with an offer to remove the "if only" from the equation.

Every day of every year, every church leader should be prepared to immediately respond to "What would you do with a million dollars if I gave it to you?"

This chapter covers most of the basics of conducting a successful campaign for those times that a full-on capital campaign is warranted. I encourage you to study those details, but if you are not in need of a campaign in the near future, you still need the dream of "if only..."

Individual Reflection

Use the space provided in this chapter to write your own thoughts and responses to the questions below. If you prefer, you can do your writing in a separate notebook or journal.

★ If you were a part of a full capital campaign where at least twice the amount of your annual budget was sought for a cause, how did it feel to wrestle with giving what for many would be their largest gift ever?

★ Did you feel that you were funding changing lives or funding brick and mortar?

★ What do you think should be done with a one-million-dollar gift to your church?

★ How did it feel to consider the possibility of using someone from outside the congregation to lead a campaign? After reading this chapter does this make sense for your church?

★ Have you known of people in your church who made significant gifts to someplace other than the church? Is there anything the church could have done to redirect such a gift—a reason so compelling that it would outshine the other cause for that giver?

★ If your church has not expressed any desire for one-time large gifts to fulfill a dream within the last five years, do you think some people in your church have simply put their gifts elsewhere?

Group Discussion

Discuss your thoughts about the questions above as a group. Depending upon the size of your group, you may want to talk in a circle or around a table all together. If more than five or six people are at this session, you might break up into groups of two to four. Share together, as you feel led, your answers to the above questions. Take about five minutes for each one.

Also, discuss as a group this question, and capture key ideas: How can a capital campaign play a valuable role in your church's Generosity Battle Plan?

Group Learning

What specifically have you learned that you want to intentionally add to your church's Generosity Plan going forward? Discuss and decide together.

PARTICIPANT HOMEWORK

★ ★

There is no Digging Deeper this week. Instead, each participant will do an extended homework activity. This activity is not based on last week's lesson but on next week's session on the Generosity Battle Plan. We are going to be taking all that we have learned and discussed and begin to formulate a concrete action plan. This plan will help us combat the material influences in our society with life-giving generosity!

Each person should write an email to the leader of this God vs. Money study. Look back over your notes from this book or your journal. In the email message, write out those things you would like to see incorporated into your church's Generosity Battle Plan. What changes do you think should be implemented? What other ideas did you come up with or record in your weekly reflections to improve the ministry of generosity in your church?

The leader should compile the ideas from all the emails and make a master list of them on a large flip chart. Then, if there are more than a dozen ideas, look for duplication and similarity between ideas, and collapse them into one category. For example, several people might suggest some sort of mission-dreaming event, such as a special worship service, all-church retreat, or prayer walk. Instead of listing each separate version, create one main idea—Dreaming Event—to list on the flip chart. Try to cull the ideas down so that there are no more than twelve to eighteen main ideas.

Write the ideas on a large flip chart sheet, using large lettering so that people can see them from everywhere in the room. Leave several inches of space between the ideas, to allow room for participants to place their votes. The leader should hang the sheet (or sheets!) on the wall of your meeting room before next week's session. This will help you make sure you do not leave something out as you start moving through the year with your Generosity Battle Plan.

Each person is also to write here or in a journal what a generous church would look like, using your church in your mission field as the example. These visions of generosity will be shared next week.

Thoroughly read and study chapter 7 of the main book.

Prayer

Most Generous Lord, once again we come with thanks and gratitude. Our pockets are full, our bellies are full, and our hearts are full because you love us. Help each of us this week to be diligent, thoughtful, and bold as we spend time thinking and praying about how to foster generosity in our congregation and how to become a church that reflects your generosity to the whole world. Amen.

Session 6

An Extended Group Session

Designing Your Church's Generosity Battle Plan

Read chapter 7 of the main book,

God vs. Money: Winning Strategies in the Combat Zone,

before this session.

This is the final session, and it is time for you to design your Generosity Battle Plan. Remember, this is not a money-raising plan. The focus is on creating generous people by helping them understand and respond to God's gracious gifts to us. It is about creating stewards, strengthening lives, and establishing a new culture within your church. If the focus shifts to just raising money, the leader must quickly remind everyone of the purpose.

I encourage your group to take a retreat for this final session. You can retreat in the church or at some other location. Ideally, you will have a day and a half together, but a full day can work well too. The main idea is to set aside ample time for this important work. The fruit it produces could change the course of your church. The initial discussion alone could take one or two hours as you hammer out the things you have learned and seek to discover how to put the best practices into play. If you chose not to retreat, then set aside a minimum of three hours for this session.

Activity Review

Each person should share briefly with the group what they wrote down in this book or in their journal about what a generous church should look like. Specifically, share your ideas about what your church will look like and be like if a culture of generosity is created. Make notes below about others' ideas that particularly spark your interest.

Watch Video 6:
Special Forces

This video covers some important final topics. This will give you food for thought and inspiration to follow through on the task of this session—designing and finalizing a yearlong Generosity Battle Plan for your church.

Notes:

Group Discussion: Prioritizing Your Ideas

Your suggestions and ideas, which you emailed to your group leader, should be written on paper flip chart sheets hanging around the room where you are gathered. Each participant should have markers, stickers, or sticky notes they can use to cast their vote on the prioritization of these ideas.

Using your voting tools, every person in the group should rank the importance of each idea or suggestion. Designate each idea as Vitally Important, Very Important, or Important.

As a group, discuss each idea and get consensus on whether to leave it in its importance category.

Next, determine whether the items you have listed should be done daily, weekly, monthly, quarterly, or annually.

Next, go through the chapter and review the suggestions for the seasons of the year, and place your plan into seasons. If you are retreating, I suggest that you pause at this point and call it a night. Give serious thought to what has been said and pray over what is being done.

Ideally, the leader and a couple of others will write out a draft of the plan now, based on the work just completed. You might use a large wall calendar, a simple Word document, or a spreadsheet—whatever works for your team. Make copies for the group before you reconvene.

The next morning (or after a break), following prayer and devotion, distribute the written draft of the plan.

Begin by asking if anyone has any additional insights into what was done the day before.

Should anything be added or subtracted?

Should greater clarity be given to any particular part?

Gain consensus on any changes, and revise the plan accordingly, adding and revising it by hand for now.

Next, take the plan segment by segment and begin to assign individuals to be accountable for each part. This does not mean that they will be the initiator or leader, only that they will be accountable to see that this particular section of the plan is done around the timeline established. It is fine for staff to have responsibilities, but it is a *must* that a layperson be assigned alongside them.

Pay particular attention to pages 80–81 in *God vs. Money: Winning Strategies in the Combat Zone*, and consider those items that should have consistent focus. These items must be done, no matter what, whether you are a small, rural church or a megachurch. These components should be nonnegotiable.

If you are retreating, I suggest you attempt to wrap up around noon with two persons assigned to write up the latest version of your Generosity Battle Plan and distribute it to participants for review. One final meeting should then be held to affirm or amend the plan before you take it forward for approval.

Additional Notes

If you are considering a major capital campaign as a part of your Generosity Battle Plan, please seek out expert counsel from professionals who work with churches on generosity and capital campaigns. A campaign will and should affect your plan, and adjustments may be called for. This can all be positive, but if handled wrongly it can have devastating consequences going forward.

If you believe it is likely that your congregation will experience a lead pastor change during the first year of your plan, adjustments may be called for. If possible, do not initiate the plan until the new pastor is on board and in full agreement with the plan.

Whenever you are seeking to change the culture of a congregation, it is helpful to have that congregation as focused as possible on the plan. If there is some internal conflict going on or a major effort on another transforming initiative, such as a new facility, hold off on your plan until these things are resolved.

I must remind you all again. This Generosity Battle Plan is a spiritual battle and not a financial one. You will likely find the focus shifting—subtly or overtly—from generosity to fundraising. This will happen intentionally, when people misunderstand the heart of the matter and try to "correct" it. It will happen subtly, in the language people reflexively use when they talk about giving. It may happen unintentionally, when words are not carefully chosen for sermons, newsletters, websites, emails, and other church communications.

Be on the lookout, and support each other's efforts to stick with your Generosity Battle Plan and to implement it with excellence. Redirect mistaken ideas, and continually replace them with careful, consistent communication of the ideas and principles reflected in your plan.

Remember, you are raising a culture of generosity. It will come from *and result in* transformed lives and renewed souls. Do not lose sight of your true mission!

Notes from Session 1

Notes from Session 2

Notes from Session 3

Notes from Session 4

Notes from Session 5

Notes from Session 6

Notes on Your
Generosity Battle Plan

CPSIA information can be obtained
at www.ICGtesting.com
Printed in the USA
LVHW081548130719
623837LV00004B/2/P